Introduction

This book seeks to promote the sexual rights of people with learning disabilities. It does this by drawing together knowledge and experience in relation to the sexuality of people with learning disabilities and sexuality more widely. It considers how services can work to promote and safeguard these rights and the responsibilities which accompany them.

What we know about sex and people with learning disabilities

Research and practice have highlighted the vulnerability of people with learning disabilities to sexual abuse and have shown how gender and power can lead to sexual exploitation. Services are now in a good position to recognise sexual abuse and respond with support and protection (Brown, Stein and Turk, 1995). We also understand more about the sexuality of people with learning disabilities (McCarthy and Thompson, 1994). Many do not have opportunities for sexual expression, but for those who do, sex is not always a mutual or enjoyable activity. The sexuality of people with learning disabilities also reflects aspects of the diversity found more widely in society. It is not uncommon for men with learning disabilities to have sex with men or for more able men to have sex outside formal support systems (Cambridge, 1996a). The issues around HIV and AIDS have also encouraged a new directness and openness when talking about sex.

In the past, the responses of services and carers to the sexuality of people with learning disabilities were often based more on stereotypes than assessed needs. People with learning disabilities were seen either as perpetual children who needed to be protected from sexual knowledge or as unable to control their sex urges. As a result, sexuality was avoided or ignored and opportunities to develop friendships and personal relationships were denied or restricted. Many staff and carers still find this a difficult need to respond to. This is despite the availability of an increasingly wide range of sex education and staff training resources and is due in part to a continuing reluctance of many in society to talk about sex. Some staff are embarrassed to talk about sex and some people with learning disabilities are ashamed or frightened to talk about ordinary sexual behaviours like masturbation or same sex relationships. Sexuality and sexual abuse policies are now becoming more common in services for people with learning disabilities and should provide practical guidance for staff to promote people's rights and develop best practice (ARC/NAPSAC 1993, Cambridge and McCarthy, 1996).

Why we need to think in terms of sexual rights

From one angle things are no different for people with learning disabilities than for anyone else. The rape and sexual exploitation of women, sexual abuse within and outside the family, homophobia, ignorance of HIV and prejudice towards people with AIDS are part of our lives or the communities in which we live. To combat these things we have fought for basic sexual rights, such as freedom from abuse and exploitation, freedom to choose a sexual partner of the same or opposite sex, information on safer sex and so on.

But human rights have traditionally been denied to people with learning disabilities, so from another angle, questions of vulnerability and patterns of occurrence make these things more important for disadvantaged groups. Some people with learning disabilities may not have the expressive language to tell others what has happened to them or the assertiveness and self confidence to say 'no' to sex they don't want. Many have also been incarcerated in large institutions for many years and remain dependent on others for basic care. Most are economically powerless and do not usually have the resources to purchase advice or pool their expertise or experience, including that about sex. Many people with learning disabilities also find it difficult to organise to demand their rights because they remain largely isolated in segregated services, despite living in the community.

Rights and empowerment

Empowerment is a difficult concept to articulate or promote, but a starting point is to be clear about the rights people have. As suggested, these are rights we should all enjoy but which many people, regardless of learning disability, are denied. Because people with learning disabilities are doubly disadvantaged, it is important to set out their basic sexual rights and to encourage a consideration of these by staff and services. A companion booklet has been produced for people with learning disabilities (McCarthy and Cambridge, 1996).

Obtaining rights is a difficult thing to do in a society and a political system which tends to avoid an explicit articulation of rights. We have an unwritten constitution and no Bill of Rights, unlike the United States of America. But we think in terms of rights and often this is linked with responsibilities such as the responsibility to protect others from sexual abuse or exploitation, to fight discrimination against gay men or lesbians and to support people with HIV or AIDS. To a degree, our rights and responsibilities are reflected in law, but we do not all have equal access to the law and the law is not applied equitably to all. Our rights are also articulated through the political process, at one level because political debate can lead to a change in the law and at another because direct action and demonstration can have an impact on the thinking and behaviour of politicians. The debates about homosexuality and abortion are good examples.

Rights and the law

The law as it applies both to sexuality and to people with learning disabilities needs to be considered in this respect. There are laws about sexuality and related matters which apply generally, such as the age of consent for homosexuality between men and the legalisation of abortion and laws which make specific reference to people with learning disabilities. Some of these laws are discriminatory and/or inconsistent and we need to acknowledge this before articulating people's sexual rights or acting to promote rights (Gunn, 1996a and b). For instance, the age of consent for homosexual sex between men is 18 and for heterosexual sex is 16, so the law is discriminatory. In its attempts to protect people with learning disabilities, the law imposes restrictions on sexual activity between some people with learning disabilities and people without learning disabilities.

Moreover, specific laws have been passed to restrict the ways local authorities present material or information relating to homosexuality, but these are discredited and unusable. Service managers are in the best position to give advice to staff on the interpretation of legislation in relation to supporting people with learning disabilities and good policies and guidelines should include key advice in those areas. Access to information can also help empower people and BILD has also published resources for staff, parents and service users on HIV and AIDS (Cambridge, 1996b, c and d) and there are similar booklets for service users on the subject of sexual abuse (Hollins and Sinason, 1993a and b).

This booklet

This booklet adopts a direct approach, drawing from sex and safer sex education, research, staff training, consultancy experience and wider debates, to identify ten important sexual rights. These can also be seen as responsibilities. For instance, the right to freedom from sexual abuse also has an equivalent responsibility not to abuse or exploit others. Services for people with learning disabilities and support staff and carers have a double responsibility, namely to uphold and safeguard the rights of other people with learning disabilities and to promote their responsibilities to others.

Responsibilities can be interpreted and exercised from the perspectives of individuals acting in socially responsible ways and from services acting in their capacity to promote freedom from oppression, individual choice and independence. The latter are attributes valued by society and the service philosophies stemming from Normalisation and Social Role Valorisation (Wolfensberger, 1980 and 1984), including an Ordinary Life (King's Fund, 1980) and the Five Accomplishments (O'Brien, 1987). Responsibilities have often been avoided because they are often seen to conflict with rights and are difficult for staff and services to practice.

This booklet now moves on to look at 10 important sexual - and by implication - other rights. They are not in any particular order of importance, as this will vary from individual to individual. They are the rights the author considers people with learning disabilities are entitled to. The reasons for each right are introduced first. These are followed by a **statement of right.** Suggestions are then made about action services, support staff and carers can take to put rights into practice and the individual responsibilities which go with rights.

1 Sexual abuse and exploitation

Sexual abuse and sexual violence are mostly experienced by women in our society and are mainly inflicted by men. They are a product of wider structural inequalities in respect of gender, power, attitudes towards women and the ways abusive behaviours are learned. These inequalities also show in the roles women are expected to adopt and their lack of political voice and economic power. People with learning disabilities are subject to sexual abuse and exploitation, again almost wholly from men without learning disabilities and more able men with learning disabilities. Imbalance in power can also be exhibited in less obvious ways such as a lack of mutuality in sex and personal relationships and what women put up with in relation to sex, such as sex which is aggressive, which hurts them or which they don't like or enjoy.

Sexual abuse is defined as sex where consent is not informed or valid (Brown and Turk, 1992). In learning disability, this means sex between two people where there are indications that one person is much more able or powerful than another and can be seen to be taking advantage. Abuse also occurs in situations in which a person has said 'no' to sex, has been unable to say 'yes' to sex or where consent has been given under pressure, with threats or bribes. Sexual abuse ranges from non-contact abuse, such as looking and verbalising, to contact abuse such as touching sexual parts and direct sexual acts. It can occur as an isolated incident or part of ongoing or ritualised abuse. (Morris, 1993).

People with learning disabilities should not have to tolerate sexual abuse or exploitation. They have a **right to freedom from sexual abuse and exploitation and to protection by services.**

This means that services should stop abuse when it happens. Suspected abuse should be reported without alerting the abuser. Opportunities for further abuse should be removed and the person abused should be protected and supported in ways which do not put them at further risk. Suspected or known abusers should not be left alone with people who they could have, or are known to have, abused. There should be guidelines for intimate personal care, staff training to help people recognise signs of abuse and procedures for reporting and managing sexual abuse.

Sexual abuse should not be tolerated even if the abuser is also a person with a learning disability - we all have a responsibility not to sexually, emotionally or physically hurt or abuse others. Sex education is needed to give people the language and safety to disclose abuse, help them understand mutuality and enable them to exercise their right to say 'no' to sex they don't want or like. Many residential services and social services departments now have policies and guidelines on sexual abuse. If your service does not have a policy and guidelines on abuse, you should push for one to be developed with staff, users and other agencies - encourage managers to commission a policy. If there is a policy and no one takes much notice of it, press for the policy to be implemented.

2 Sexual expression and relationships

Sexual expression is a normal and everyday part of life, even if some people are not sexually active through circumstance or choice. People express their sexuality in different ways, including affection, holding, intimate touching and kissing, and various sexual acts. Some people have sex outside relationships, some only within a relationship and others choose the emotional support and closeness of a relationship without sex. Different arrangements suit different people. The conventional view is that frequent sex with different people is bad, which is why terms like permissiveness are associated with negative values.

Casual sex, or having sex with a number of different sexual partners is seen by some people as wrong, whereas others consider a live-in relationship, marriage or monogamy to be restricting. Our attitudes to sexuality are influenced by our experiences and how we are socialised into thinking what is good or bad. Cultural and social factors, such as religion and political belief also influence sexual attitudes and morality. The starting point is to accept that we all have different sexual needs, feelings and preferences and express these in different ways.

People with learning disabilities are entitled to express themselves sexually. They have a **right to support which recognises their sexual needs and helps them respond in a variety of appropriate ways.**

This does not mean support for abusive, violent or other inappropriate sexual behaviours, such as masturbation in a public place where other people could be offended. Rather, it means that services should help people to develop their sexuality in ways which they like and which are appropriate in a culturally diverse society. For example: providing education and support for someone choosing to have a variety of sexual partners, without making them feel bad; helping two people to live together if they have expressed such a desire; providing a private place for someone to masturbate.

Staff should provide help within agreed programmes and plans, with the support of their manager or care manager. Practice guidelines are essential if staff are to be able to do this confidently. A useful starting point for assessing mutuality in sexual and other relationships, such as for people with limited expressive communication, is to observe whether the two people like being with each other or whether one person is more forceful than the other. It is important that interventions are appropriate - stopping someone masturbating in a living room is very different from stopping someone masturbating in the privacy of their own bedroom.

3 Same sex relationships

The politics of sexuality, including that in learning disability, now includes feminist, lesbian and gay issues. The feminist movement has affected the perception of female sexuality and helped articulate the sexual rights of women. Gay and lesbian politics has helped focus on ways to fight AIDS and the oppression resulting from homophobia. Gay, lesbian and bisexual identities are now part of the sexual diversity of Western society, although legal and social discrimination remains in Britain.

There is evidence from sexual health outreach work, sex education and needs assessment in HIV and learning disability (Cambridge, 1996a) that it is not uncommon for men with learning disabilities to have sex with men, sometimes in public places. There is also evidence from sex education that lesbian sex is uncommon for women with learning disabilities. It should not be assumed that men with learning disabilities who have sex with men identify themselves as gay. A gay identity and lifestyle is not usually accessible to men with learning disabilities. Most men with learning disabilities have been socialised into a heterosexual identity.

People with learning disabilities should not have to tolerate abuse or discrimination on the basis of their sexuality. They have a **right to same sex relationships and sexual expression and support in relation to such choices.**

This means that services have a responsibility to ensure positive attitudes and responses to minority sexual choices made by people with learning disabilities. Homophobic (as with racist) attitudes and abuse should not be tolerated by service users or staff. Sometimes staff may not be aware of the sexual feelings of the people they support and service users may pick up negative attitudes from listening to conversations or comments. On a practical level, this means treating homosexual and lesbian friendships and relationships in the same way as those between women and men. What makes sex or a relationship valid is mutuality and consent, not the gender of the people concerned. Services should make every effort to help partners live together if they have expressed a wish to do so, regardless of gender.

Services which provide support and respond to the preferences and needs of individuals are not breaking the law. Section 28 of the 1988 Local Government Act is an unworkable piece of homophobic legislation. The legal age of consent for homosexual sex has changed from 21 to 18 while the equivalent age of consent for heterosexual sex has remained at 16. Anal sex between consenting men in private is not illegal (and neither is it now between a man and a woman). Most services or agencies have equal opportunities policies and most of these include direct or indirect reference to sexual orientation. Sexuality policies will indicate that same sex relationships should be supported in the same ways as opposite sex relationships.

It is, however, unlikely to be appropriate to introduce users to the gay scene on the assumption that they will be accepted - a befriending scheme with a gay organisation might well be a better option to explore.

4 Sex education

The issues which surround sex education in schools are similar to those which have been raised in services for people with learning disabilities. A reactionary view is that sex education encourages people to have sex. A radical view is that sex education arms people with the information they need to make informed choices about sex and better understand the possible consequences. Without sex education people will explore their sexuality, so it is common sense to facilitate the safe and enjoyable aspects of sex. Myth and ignorance are dangerous because they make people more vulnerable to abuse, exploitation and sexually transmitted diseases.

Sex education for people with learning disabilities has been ignored for too long, sometimes because staff are embarrassed or do not know how to approach it. Sometimes carers, staff or managers are frightened of the consequences, because providing sex education also demands ongoing support for sex and personal relationships. Increasingly, services are adopting a proactive approach to providing sex education as sexuality policies and specialist training for educators become more usual and the benefits become more apparent.

People with learning disabilities are entitled to know about their bodies and how they work. They have a **right to sex education and services have a responsibility to provide or arrange this.**

This does not mean that sex education should be provided outside individual programmes or assessed needs. Sex education groups (McCarthy and Thompson, 1992) are a useful starting point, but membership of such groups should not vary too much in terms of skills or experience and some planning work will be needed to ensure groups are balanced. Same sex groups are also recommended because the issues discussed will not always be the same and the experiences of men and women differ. Sometimes group work will lead to personal disclosure which will justify one-to-one sex education or counselling. Procedures for delivering sex educational responses, including planning for individual needs, should be outlined in sexuality policies (Cambridge and McCarthy, 1996).

Individual sex education is valuable for developing a two way relationship of trust and for the development of individual strategies and responses. A good starting point is to respond to any questions people ask about sex in a way which encourages openness and honesty and which reinforces the message that good sex and consenting sex is OK. The subject of sex can also be approached by talking about body parts and names and the differences between men and women. Potential conflicts of interest, such as confidentiality, will need to be addressed beforehand, but good sex educators address confidentiality from the outset. There is now a wide choice of sex education resources available to help work with people with learning disabilities (see resource list), including videos, line drawings and examples of peer education (People First, 1994).

5 HIV, AIDS and sexual health

When AIDS was first recognised it was thought to be mainly associated with gay men, because of a combination of myth and homophobia. AIDS is caused by the HIV virus and is mainly transmitted by blood and semen. Although in Britain HIV mainly affects men who have sex with men, in different parts of the world it is also particularly associated with heterosexual transmission through anal or vaginal sex. Mothers with HIV can transmit infection to their babies although this does not happen in the majority of cases. In some cities, HIV is associated with injecting drug use. The use of dirty (shared) needles and works (drug injecting equipment) for injecting drugs and unprotected anal and vaginal sex (penetrative sex without a condom) all carry a high risk of transmitting HIV. Safer sex and the use of condoms for anal and vaginal sex protect against HIV infection. It also helps protect against other sexually transmitted diseases including syphilis, gonorrhea, NSU and herpes.

During the early 1990s AIDS was 're-gayed' in recognition of the fact that about 70% of those affected were men who had sex with men. This was the group where resources such as HIV prevention and support for people with HIV and AIDS needed to be directed. Effective education and information has focused on presenting safer sex as empowering, with positive images of homosexuality. There has been a reluctance to tackle HIV head-on in learning disability services although accounts of therapy (Morris, 1996) and sex education (Thompson, 1994) suggest that HIV risk also lies with men with learning disabilities who have sex with men. This is where resources, including safer sex education should be targeted, although educators should aim to integrate safer sex work with sex education more widely, including information about other sexually transmitted diseases.

People with learning disabilities are entitled to information about HIV and other sexually transmitted infections and how to protect themselves. They have a **right to safer sex education, access to condoms and the support required to practice safer sex.**

A first step is to provide support for sexual relationships in open and constructive ways, including sexual relationships between men with learning disabilities and other men. All people with learning disabilities receiving sex education or who are sexually active, should know about sexually transmitted diseases and their main symptoms and have prompt access to medical help via a GUM clinic or their GP, should they need it. Services also have a responsibility to ensure that people do not experience discrimination on the basis of their suspected or known HIV status, such as being excluded from services or staff support. Confidentiality should also be maintained. There is no significant risk of HIV transmission through social care procedures. The BILD booklet for staff on HIV and AIDS cover these points in more detail (Cambridge, 1996c).

Services and commissioners should develop risk assessment and risk management skills in relation to HIV (Cambridge, 1996e). In the first instance, this does not mean policing sexual behaviour or prohibiting sexual activity, but helping facilitate an informed understanding of risk and reducing high risk behaviour through educational and support interventions. These include counselling and therapy on an individual and group basis and explaining responsibilities to prevent the transmission of HIV and other sexually transmitted diseases. Providing free access to condoms demonstrates a commitment to safer sex but does not guarantee their use. HIV testing is generally not a solution to managing HIV risk. People should be discouraged from taking an HIV test until the possible consequences are understood and valid consent has been ascertained. Informed consent should be assessed independently of the service by specialist workers in HIV and learning disability or by competent counsellors at a GUM clinic. Unless consent is valid an HIV test amounts to assault (Gunn, 1996b).

6 Confidentiality

Confidentiality is a concept which is central to the values of Western society and reflects the high status given to privacy and individuality. Each of us have public and private spheres to our lives and behaviours and the degree to which we allow them to overlap is usually a matter of choice. The failure of individuals or communities to be clear about where such boundaries and interests lie can lead to 'in the public interest' disclosures of private affairs, where wider questions of political or economic accountability are concerned. For instance, contradictions arise when a public figure preaches family values and is later found to be having illicit sex or an extra-marital relationship, or a politician promotes his financial interests through the privileges of public office.

Health and social care services have to manage similar boundaries between wider interests and individual rights. The details held on computer records or client files kept on service users are accessed by a number of staff, professionals and managers, but some of the information may be personal. Assessment and planning for individual needs is an example. Information disclosed during sex education is a particularly powerful example, as it clearly concerns intimate details about a person's life or behaviour. If people break confidentiality or disclose private information, we have social controls we can exert and can occasionally take legal measures, such as under the Data Protection Act. There are also issues of professionalism and best practice which should guide the handling and disclosure of information in services for people with learning disabilities.

People with learning disabilities are entitled to confidentiality in their personal and private lives. They have a **right to confidentiality regarding information about their sexuality and personal relationships.**

This means not disclosing personal details to staff or other service users, or talking about people behind their backs. If a service user talks about masturbation or a same sex encounter during a one-to-one sex education session and this is disclosed to support staff, then this breaks confidentiality. Confidentiality should be assumed in such circumstances and good sex education or any other personal work should involve clarification about boundaries for confidentiality before work starts. Confidentiality does not mean keeping quiet about situations where other interests are apparent, such as sexual abuse or exploitation. In such situations services also have a responsibility to provide care and protection. An example where confidentiality can be 'managed', rather than strictly broken, relates to the disclosure of unsafe sex with someone who is assessed to be at high HIV risk.

Risk can be managed by reinforcing the importance of safer sex and working intensively with the individual without disclosing the reasons. Guidelines for managing confidential information are essential in this respect and good policies should include clear 'need to know' criteria. They might also include a named person whose advice and support could be sought in situations where interests appear to diverge. Such a person would be in a position to take up relevant issues with service managers, keyworkers, care managers or outside advice agencies in ways which do not disclose personal information or identify the individual. Confidentiality takes on added importance in relation to known HIV status and the potential consequences of breaking confidentiality about a person's HIV positive status. Similarly, the consequences of the person themself telling other people about their condition should be understood by all involved.

7 Dignity and respect

Part of feeling valued as a person is to receive recognition of your individuality and to have your preferences and choices acknowledged. This is important in relation to interactions with friends and in sexual and personal relationships. While it is unusual to find any relationship which is totally balanced, there will often be elements of inter-dependence and mutuality. When power and control are heavily imbalanced, abuse or violence can often occur. It is easy for others to devalue people's dignity and respect when they are not politically powerful or perceived to be productive economically or socially. People without a stake in society easily become marginalised and excluded from decision making and wider political participation.

People with learning disabilities are usually excluded from making decisions about their lives in everyday matters and major life defining events (see the Five Accomplishments, O'Brien, 1987). This explains the development of concepts like user involvement and participation as routes to empowerment for people with learning disabilities. Empowerment has been difficult to establish because people with learning disabilities still depend on services and staff support for many things other people take for granted, such as participation, mobility and personal and intimate care. Dependency remains despite the 1990 community care reforms which promoted consumerism, choice and user involvement. The introduction of contracts and market forces in social care has failed to liberate people who use services from institutionalised support and dependency relationships.

People with learning disabilities are entitled to be treated as individuals with choices and feelings. They have a **right to live with dignity and to be treated with respect, particularly during intimate care.**

This means that services should work with people as individuals and staff should not impose their own values or beliefs. This is difficult to do because service users often ask staff what they think. Giving an opinion and the reasons for it, is different from saying something is right or wrong when it relates to people's lifestyles or preferences, including their sexual choices. Referencing principles like the Five Accomplishments can help provide a framework for action, but like Normalisation, these can be difficult to interpret and put into practice. Most importantly, services should create the spaces and opportunities to consult with service users individually and collectively. Individual planning meetings, user's forums and self advocacy are examples. Organisations run by people with learning disabilities, like People First, can provide advice and there may be local branches. There are also a few examples of peer sex education services.

People need to be encouraged to understand their situations, the options they face and to act in their own interests. This may mean ending a sexual relationship which hurts them or starting a new relationship which holds emotional risks. In relation to competence, people need to develop skills that are functional and attributes which decrease dependency. This may mean asserting their preferences for certain types of sex in a relationship rather than putting up with things they don't like. Women with learning disabilities need particular encouragement and support to be more assertive. Part of the answer is to help people develop a positive self image through workshops and one-to-one support. Allowing people to choose a keyworker or same sex staff member for intimate care are further examples of how services can work towards promoting dignity, respect and choice.

8 Privacy

From one angle, considerations of privacy mirror those of confidentiality, for they are concerned with the boundaries between public and private domains. People who work and have their own homes constantly cross between public and private worlds. At work they are usually in public or collective domains and at home they are usually in private domains, shared with partners, relatives or friends. Social trends suggest society is moving further from congregate living, for instance in large family units, to small or single person households, with parallel trends in employment and the distribution of income and wealth. Society has become more individualistic, with a tendency to invest in private wealth and disinvest in public space and services.

There have been parallel trends in services for people with learning disabilities. Deinstitutionalisation has meant moving from congregate and large scale services like hospitals, dormitories and hostels to ordinary and small scale units like houses, flats and home care placements. Segregation has been replaced by attempts at social integration in wider communities, with more individualisation and less congregation. With these changes have come greater opportunities for privacy in the lives of people with learning disabilities, reflecting wider societal values. Privacy in sexual matters and relationships has been given increased prominence as private space like bedrooms become more available for people with learning disabilities.

People with learning disabilities are entitled to have private spaces of their own to use alone or with a friend or sexual partner. They have **a right to privacy in their personal and sexual lives.**

This means single bedrooms should be provided and, where this is an expressed preference, services should strive to achieve this objective. This is not necessarily easy to do as it has cost implications, but is a key step in improving the quality of people's lives and environments. Some people express a preference to share bedrooms with a friend and this is fine. The important thing is that people's choices are informed and taken seriously. It may be appropriate for people to have locks on their doors to protect and reinforce their privacy or to have their own front door keys. Services should also plan to implement these basic steps. Some people may wish to have their own flats or accommodation shared with friends.This is another way in which people who are independent enough to live with low staff support may achieve privacy. There are many other ways services can help people acquire life and self-care skills, such as education and employment programmes.

This is not the same as leaving people unsupported on their own, ignoring their needs or allowing risk situations to develop. Such neglect was a common feature of the old large institutions like hospitals and some hostels. Staff interaction with residents and user participation and engagement in activities is generally much higher in community settings (Mansell et al, 1987). When keyworking and programmed activities are employed with service users, a balance can be struck between providing opportunities for privacy while maintaining access to shared formal and informal activities, interaction and engagement. At the same time, it is important that staff respect the privacy of service users and that service users respect the privacy of the people they live or share with. People should be allowed to retreat to their bedrooms when they wish to be alone and should respect other people's private space.

9 Pornography and sexual aids

Pornography is a product of a society which commercialises sex and other human behaviours. People profit from sex by producing written, pictorial and video material which is sexually explicit and designed and marketed for the purpose of sexual gratification. The political and moral debate about pornography hinges on the exploitation and degradation of women and children. Links have also been made between pornography and sexual violence and the sexual corruption of younger people. The debate about pornography also includes questions about freedom of choice and access to information, choice to work in the sex industry and policing the use and exchange of sexually explicit material. It is mainly men who buy and use pornography, whether men or women are depicted. Some men with learning disabilities also use pornography.

Many of the questions about pornography are relevant to support services for people with learning disabilities. Sexually explicit material is sometimes needed for sex education, but there is an important difference between the two. Erotic images also have the potential to be misinterpreted in sex education. The use of vibrators or other devices for sexual stimulation to help with masturbation, sometimes raise similar concerns. We are all bombarded by sexually explicit and erotic images from advertising, and soft pornography is readily available from newsagents. People with learning disabilities are not insulated from these things and will also encounter such images. The choice to buy erotic or pornographic material exists for some people with learning disabilities.

People with learning disabilities should not be excluded from the choices available to other people. They have **a right to buy and use pornography or sexual aids and to education about their use.**

This means helping people to use pornography as an aid to sexual gratification in an appropriate private place. An example would be to gain sexual stimulation from looking at pornography as a means to achieve orgasm during masturbation in a bedroom. Services have a responsibility to help ensure pornography is used only in private and users have a responsibility not to impose it on other people who use or work in services. The management of pornography should be part of an agreed individual programme relating to support for sexuality. Staff should not introduce service users to pornographic material under any circumstances, as it is not a substitute for proper sex education materials. Such action could easily be interpreted as abusive and could have unintended consequences and effects on the individual.

If staff are in a position to influence the nature of the material or object, careful consideration should be given to any intervention. Taking pornography away could seriously affect other behaviours. Like any product, there are good and bad examples in relation to intended use. Some pornography puts people in positions of degradation or depicts sexual violence and should be strongly discouraged. The representation of stylised or fetishised sex also presents potential problems. There is a difference between sado-masochism as part of a consenting sexual repertoire and brutal images in a pornographic magazine or video. Such images are potentially confusing to a person with a learning disability. It is also important to recognise that people who use pornography, including people with learning disabilities, have a responsibility not to impose it on other people and to keep it and use it in a private place where it will not offend others. Staff may need to provide guidance and support to achieve this.

10 Reproduction and contraception

Reproductive rights and contraception continue to trigger fierce debate and controversy. One reason is that access to contraception is perceived to encourage sexual activity, particularly in younger people. Related issues also emerge, such as parents' 'right to know' and the young person's right to confidentiality in their relationship with their GP or family planning adviser. The availability of the female contraceptive pill revolutionised the sexual and lifestyle choices available to women. There has also been a parallel debate about the morality of abortion and the right of women to choose to terminate a pregnancy. The debates about abortion and contraception have consequently included a host of social, moral and legal considerations.

People with learning disabilities have largely been excluded from the wider social debate and the choices available to women. Services have tended to manage the sexuality of people with learning disabilities outside the provision of choices and recognition of individual rights. Women with learning disabilities who were sexually active were routinely sterilised without their informed consent. A High Court judgement is now required for this to happen. The sexual activities of men with learning disabilities were also routinely managed by drugs which suppressed their sexual feelings. Women were frequently put on the contraceptive pill. Although drugs are still directly and indirectly prescribed to men and women with learning disabilities for such purposes, the predominant view is that this is unacceptable practice for managing sexual activity or its consequences.

People with learning disabilities are entitled to have advice and information on contraception and reproduction. They have **a right to counselling for reproduction and to choose and practice contraception.**

Women and men with learning disabilities should receive information about contraception as part of sex education. Women with learning disabilities who require contraception should be helped to make an informed choice based on the advantages and disadvantages of each option. Longer-term sexual partners should be encouraged to take the woman's preferences into account and, where necessary, take or share responsibility for contraception. While the use of condoms is likely to be unreliable, they also offer protection against HIV and other sexually transmitted diseases. No form of contraception should be used against the expressed wishes of the woman concerned and sterilisation should only be undertaken with the informed consent of the woman, independently assessed by specialist sex education workers or competent family planning practitioners.

The use of drugs to control or manage the sexual behaviour of men with learning disabilities should be discouraged as this can have wider physical and emotional side effects and does not tackle the individual or environmental factors contributing to the behaviour. Where possible, the sexual partners of women with learning disabilities should be involved in decisions about contraception and reproduction to help ensure that all practical options have been explored. Termination of pregnancy should be open to women with learning disabilities as with other women but should only be undertaken on the basis of the informed choice of the woman or for over-riding medical or health reasons. People with learning disabilities who have expressed a wish to have children should be supported to consider and plan reproduction and child-rearing through independent counselling. Services should be prepared to plan for and support such changing needs.

Conclusion

The articulation of sexual rights is difficult and opens one up to criticism on a number of fronts. Some people will respond that promoting rights brings unacceptable risks or is irresponsible. Others will not agree with particular rights or the ways suggested to implement them. Ultimately, rights and sexual morality is a matter of opinion and personal choice. I would argue that choice is the key consideration here. For too long people with learning disabilities who are capable of making informed choices with guidance and support have been denied such opportunities. In the process, they have also been denied their sexuality. The task facing services and staff is to uphold people's rights, facilitate informed choice and explain equivalent responsibilities and possible consequences. This may be especially difficult for people with profound learning disabilities who usually have everyday and life-defining choices made for them, which is why they are easy targets for all forms of abuse. But unless we identify such aims we will never be in a position to reach for them. Open and informed discussion itself is a starting point for changes in attitude and behaviour.

References

ARC/NAPSAC (1993)
It could never happen here! The prevention and treatment of sexual abuse of adults with learning disabilities in residential settings
ARC/NAPSAC Chesterfield

Brown, H., Stein, J., and Turk, V (1995)
The sexual abuse of adults with learning disabilities:
report of a second two year incidence survey
Mental Handicap Research, Vol.8, No.1, 3-24

Brown, H and Turk, V (1992)
Defining sexual abuse as it affects adults with learning disabilities
Mental Handicap, Vol.20, 2, 44-55

Cambridge, P (1996a)
Men with learning disabilities who have sex with men in public places: mapping the needs of services and users in south east London
Journal of Intellectual Disability Research (in press)

Cambridge, P (1996b, c and d)
HIV and AIDS and people with learning disabilities: what you need to know about HIV and AIDS/Guidelines for staff and carers/A guide for parents
BILD, Kidderminster.

Cambridge, P (1996e)
Assessing and meeting needs in HIV and learning disability
British Journal of Learning Disability (in press)

Cambridge, P and McCarthy, M (1996)
Developing and implementing sexuality policy for a learning disability provider service,
Health and Social Care in the Community (in press)

Gunn, M (1996a)
Sex and the Law: A brief guide for staff working with people with learning disabilities
FPA, London (in press)

Gunn, M (1996)
The Law, HIV and people with learning disabilities, in (Eds.) P. Cambridge and H. Brown
HIV and Learning Disabilities
BILD, Kidderminster (in press)

Hollins, S and Sinason, V (1993a)
Bob Tells All
St George's Mental Health Library, London.

Hollins, S and Sinason, V (1993b)
Jenny Speaks Out
St George's Mental Health Library, London.

King's Fund (1980)
An ordinary Life: Comprehensive locally-based residential services for mentally handicapped people
King's Fund Centre, London.

Mansell, J., Felce, D., Jenkins, J., de Kock U and Toogood, S (1987)
Developing staffed housing for people with mental handicaps
Costello, Tunbridge Wells.

Morris. S (1993)
Protect and Survive
Community Care, 30 December, pp 12-13.

Morris, S (1996)
Experiences of Risk: The role of therapy in sexual health, in (Eds.) P. Cambridge and H. Brown
HIV and Learning Disabilities
BILD, Kidderminster. (in press)

McCarthy, M and Cambridge, P (1996)
Your Rights about Sex: a booklet for people with learning disabilities
BILD, Kidderminster.

McCarthy, M and Thompson, D (1992)
Sex and the 3 Rs: Rights, Responsibilities and Risks
Pavilion, Brighton.

McCarthy, M and Thompson, D (1994)
HIV/AIDS and safer sex work with people with learning disabilities, in (Ed.) A. Craft,
Practice issues in Sexuality and Learning Disabilities
Routledge, London.

O'Brien, J (1987)
A Guide to lifestyle planning: Using the activities catalogue to integrate services and natural support systems, in (Eds.) B. Willcox and G. Bellamy
The Activities Catalogue: an alternative curriculum for youth and adults with severe disabilities
Brookes, Baltimore.

People First (1994)
Everything you ever wanted to know about safer sex but nobody bothered to tell you
People First, London.

Thompson, D (1994)
Sexual experiences and sexual identity for men with learning disabilities who have sex with men
Changes, Vol. 12, No.4.

Turk, V and Brown, H (1993)
The sexual abuse of adults with learning disabilities: Results of a two year incidence survey
Mental Handicap Research, Vol.6, No.3, 193-216

Wolfensberger, W (1980)
The Definition of Normalisation: Update, problems, disagreements and misunderstandings, in (Eds.) R. Flynn and K. Nitsch,
Normalisation, social integration and community services,
University Park Press, Baltimore.

Wolfensberger, W (1984)
A Reconception of Normalisation as Social Role Valorisation,
Mental Retardation (Canadian) 34, 22-5.

Key resources

Cambridge, P (1996b, c and d)
HIV and AIDS and people with learning disabilities: What you need to know about HIV and AIDS/Guidelines for staff and carers/Guide for parents
BILD, Kidderminster.

FPANSW (1993)
Feeling Sexy. Feeling Safe
Family Planning Association of New South Wales. A video using actors for safer sex and scenes from sex education and social situations.

McCarthy, M and Cambridge, P (1996)
Your Rights about Sex: a booklet for people with learning disabilities
BILD, Kidderminster.

McCarthy, M and Thompson, D (1992)
Sex and the 3 Rs: Rights, Responsibilities and Risks.
Pavilion, Brighton. Educational materials including line drawings.

SELHPS (1992)
My Choice, My Own Choice
South East London Health Promotion Service, Pavilion Publishing, Brighton. A video
acted by people with learning disabilities focusing on the social and consent aspects to sex
and personal relationships.

WLHPA (1994)
Piece by Piece
West London Health Promotion Agency. A video with sequences of sex, personal hygiene and
social situations using puppets.